ABOUT THE AUTHOR

Ana Seferović, a Belgrade born writer living in London, has written four books of poetry, all published in Serbia. This is her first solo collection in English.

Her poetry has been translated and published in many languages. She is also a co-author of two published and staged plays.

She was and is engaged in numerous cross-over art/poetry projects in collaboration with various poets, musicians and visual artists.

She is forever in love with palm trees.

ABOUT *MATERINA*

'The real hero/ine of Ana Seferovic's MATERINA is 'Everyone' an anonymous daily character whom we met in *Pilgrim's Progress* or in Chaucer's *Canterbury Tales*: the hero is a working boy or a girl who needs a line of coke to set herself free; the hero here is a city, overtime and angry consciousness, coupling with the notion of a hardworking migrant living his exodus to the brim. There is no leisure or free time in the book where a migrant could breathe. S/he barely has time to remember where he came from, namely from MATERINA which is a multilayered notion, in Serbian it stands for the place of birth or one's origin, but in larger argotic idiom it denotes "no place", non-lieu or a local Hell where the speaker verbally sends his brother to when he wants to get rid of him. Almost 'everyone' can go back to their own 'materina', but not the migrant, to his colossal body of his country stricken by war. A migrant can only go back to his/her memories; if these don't destroy us, they always make us stronger, and Seferovic's poetry interwoven with memories here has become stronger and harder metaphor than the one we read in the beginning of her work. Powder sugar on the cake of her early work has crystalized into a very strong, unbreakable substance that only an indomitable pen, like her own, is able to describe and carry one. Art could be seen, she says as 'incompetence at life'. **Nina Zivancevic**

'The poems in na Seferovic's *Materina* address multiple layers of what both 'mother' and 'motherland' mean, with new meaning refracted when these are located within the context of war and migration. The altered/ altering body which does not belong -'(one day it will perfect, just perfect!)' - and felt only in relation to another body. Generational trauma and inherited memory hang in rarefied and exquisite exhibition which Seferovic journeys through via internal and external perceptions, which themselves are constantly breaking down - 'The border was an obsessive idea: parents trashing maps, drawing new imaginary borders in the air.' Whilst the employed form holds great tension, the reader is air-borne via stunning archetypal contemplation of the everyday - 'the moon was a rounded scarab with golden vibrating wings.' Subtle layers amount to a work resonant of Calvino's *Invisible Cities* with the additional intrusions/ escape of a digital world - the whole device articulating with a singular feminist analysis of (and witness to) war. As such, this is a radical literary contribution. Experientially, to enter a Seferovic poem is akin to walking around a museum of dreams with sharp curatorial style and analysis. Always political, unfailingly humane and often funny, Seferovic holds a unique voice and space in contemporary poetics - 'all would be better without sound - switch it off!' **Rushika Wick**

MATERINA
Ana Seferović

VERVE
POETRY PRESS
BIRMINGHAM

PUBLISHED BY VERVE POETRY PRESS
https://vervepoetrypress.com
mail@vervepoetrypress.com

All rights reserved
© 2023 Ana Seferović

The right of Ana Seferović to be identified as author of this work has been asserted in accordance with section 77 of the Copyright, Designs and Patents Act 1988.

No part of this work may be reproduced, stored or transmitted in any form or by any means, graphic, electronic, recorded or mechanical, without the prior written permission of the publisher.

FIRST PUBLISHED JULY 2023

Printed and bound in the UK
by ImprintDigital, Exeter

ISBN: 978-1-913917-39-5

PREFACE

'

Materina started as an exploration of the Balkan wars of the '90s through a feminist lens, but became a document of a wider trauma.

In Serbian there is no word for Motherland, only Fatherland, and I wanted to tell a story about a Motherland (not a Fatherland) - an unofficial history of the other, of the outcast by default, about war from a different perspective, about pain that lingers through generations and about the cruelty of freedom once achieved. Even if there was a word for Motherland, motherland is always something other than Fatherland, it's the other, it's the unofficial, it's the undocummented.

I had two files while working on the book, one in Serbian and one in English. Sometimes I would write in Serbian, sometimes in English, depending on a mood, but then I had to translate bits I wrote in English to Serbian and vice versa, plus many edits, so each line is translated at least twice from one language to another. The book is unusual in that way: there is no original language of the book, both Serbian and English are translations created simultaneously, the translations *are* the originals, there is no official language of Materina. And that is perfect given that I am an immigrant someone in-between borders, cultures and languages. I live in that no-man's land. Also we are all translations, constantly translating ourselves to others.

There is no word for Motherland but there is a word Materina. Materina is a special form of genitive of the noun majka (mother), mostly used in swear words, for example: Go back to materina (go back to your mother's _____ (the swear word cu*t is omitted)) or when you want to say that someone is from some horrible small town you say: oh they are from materina. I wanted to reclaim the word Materina and write poem-stories from that unofficial history of Materina, whose borders do not belong to just one country or nation. It's a no-man's land. And therefore names of places and countries are omitted. These are stories from that no-mans land about people who don't belong anywhere.

Ana Seferovic, July 2023

CONTENTS

Preface

Falling Bodies	13
Here: The Conspiracy of Quasi Temporality	25
And You Shine Content	31
While the World Was Disappearing, We Grew and Grew	39
Until Such Time Reality Is Just an Abstraction	49
The Doll's Game	57
You Should Show that Love Sometimes	59
This Is the Colour of Happiness	65
The Past Is a Grotesque Animal*	69
The Future Is an Animal Dancing in a Coffee Cup	71
Freedom Throws the Prescribed Tomorrow Down the Mountain	73
If Only You Could Have Seen Those Divine Herons	77
Hide and Seek	107
Do Your Thing, Storm	127

Acknowledgements

MATERINA

Falling Bodies

They met up in a hotel room

He rented it for a night

On a table, a bottle of whiskey and few lines of coke were waiting for her

This is good, she thought

She feels strong repulsion towards naked bodies

Towards hers as well

Drugs, drinks do help —

Mastering repulsion

First things first

First hate you learn from your mother

And her mother hated so good, so many things-

Men—she said¬—too big of a presence—occupying too much space—their legs wide spread across the chairs—their smells—their noises...

She hated bodily functions—nobody should know you have

those¬—and she always ate alone

She hated neighbours and flies and hairs and pigeons and her father and sometimes her mother

She hated strongly the president and the government and any kind of system

She hated the church—I might change my mind if a woman becomes a Patriarch, but I don't think so, I am nobody's rib!
And she hated the winter—I will get myself arrested—heating is better in jail!
Sometimes, she hated summer as well—the exuberance, the fuss, the sun
(Elaborate and relentless agenda of opening and shutting the windows and blinds throughout the day)
And she hated people who talk too much, especially in certain languages
And people who were walking too slow; she hated untidiness and people who do not hate

She was constantly talking about Sparta:
"In Sparta, they would have thrown me off a cliff a long time ago!
Soft is the tit of our civilisation!
Nurturing idiots!
But at the end, you know—
What we deserve, that will decompose us!"

She was snorting cocaine from the table, thinking about her mother and about Sparta.

He approached her from behind and started to lift her skirt and pull down her tights

He managed to make her interested

He entered her while she was still snorting the lines

Oh, you are so dirty!

Before, she thought she was good in bed—now, that is not important to her

He put cocaine on her lips and then licked it off

She didn't want to do the same to him; he wasn't insisting

She was happy about it

She was covered in his sweat

Drops from his soaked hair were dripping into her mouth

She didn't like that

He was slippery and nervous
She was bored and tired

It all felt like such hard work
She wanted him to come, to stop, to end this funny human activity
Partly
Partly she wanted to come
That would not happen
That rarely happens
Finally it was over; she turned around and pretended she fell asleep
In the morning they were drinking coffee, nicely dressed; they were human beings again
He looked nice
He walked her to the station
I don't want to see him again. I don't want to see anybody
In the train, she felt her buttocks pleasantly aching, firm from

the all-night sex
She was content
Sex is good for you
Sex improves immune system
Makes you confident

Gets you places

Burns calories

Makes you fit

Sex makes you worthy

All those slightly gross naked foreign bodies

Dry and thirsty

All these

Working bodies

Commuting bodies

Earning bodies

Eating bodies

Writing poetry bodies

Pregnant bodies

Disabled bodies

Sleeping bodies

All those temporary bodies in a constant reshaping towards death

Could you ride all those bodies?

She looked down the carriage: faces, stomachs, groins

Yes, I probably could
It is strange how we are made—
To need each other in this way
She left her country long time ago—
An immigrant;
And that's it!
Enough
Enough for her for this life
But it was good. Happiness is banality. It is common places:
She came with a small bag; she was sleeping in corridors, churches, on sofas, on benches
Anywhere she could fit
She was working on markets, sometimes as a cleaner, as a babysitter
As a dog walker, as anything you want
Life was getting better
The lights were shining bright
She was even in a film once
Not a bad film

Parties were great, gay clubs even better

Once she met a famous musician, he even invited her for a ride in his pink convertible

They were driving along a street full of clubs and people were waving to them, she felt that

At that moment her life was going somewhere

Going somewhere big time

Going somewhere in style

In a big pink convertible

But nothing much happened

She got tired and closed her doors

Used up all the excuses why she can't go out—people left her alone at the end

She started to gather objects, from charity shops, one-pound shops, stuff she would find on the streets

Things people were throwing away

After a while, it was impossible to invite anybody to her flat—it was overcrowded from the floor to the ceiling. The only way to move around was through narrow corridors and paths in between piles of objects

At one point, she did have somebody
For some reason, he thought that all those piles of unidentified objects were

an art installation, her ongoing project
She said nothing to undeceive him
It was beautiful that somebody saw her incompetence at life as an art form

After all I am an artist! I am my own work of art!

The relationship was dragging
She got pregnant
Pregnancy was a horrifying prospect
But she decided to keep the child
Like jumping from a cliff
That was the feeling
They tried to stay together and made another child

Life became a relentless routine
They didn't last

"At least you managed to multiply" — her mother said

She even had a pet dog from a rescue centre—
We will go to a proper walk tomorrow, I promise you—she was telling the same sentence to the dog almost every day
The animal stayed un-rescued
Instead, she would go to meet men, sometimes women

All sorts of men

All sorts of women

The ones she did love

And the ones she didn't love

Fascinated with differences, with uncountable variations of always the same

Mesmerised with possibilities

She loved totally incompatible people (who knew that right away; she knew that as well right away, just couldn't resist)

And couldn't focus (on herself)

The only thing she could do for hours was drinking or sleeping

(sometimes with somebody but only with pauses)

She started to fantasize how she would go back to her mother country and reinvent herself as a farmer

She will never go back, she will never be a farmer

She doesn't even understand what all those people are doing in all those offices, in all those tall, glittery buildings...

She doesn't understand jobs or job ads
She does, but...

It was warm and humid
Morning breaths
The train
The rhythm of movement—light flickering
The head is falling down, then goes up again
I could be any story from this train I could be with anybody on this train
This train... The train of events
Everything just happened
By itself
It happened
And that is me
That thing that happened
Who am I?
Am I this name glued to this inferior ID?
Love...?
School?
What school, my dear
No school

Schools are for them

To tame them and train them to rule the world

And what did I learn in my school?
Where are the palm trees?

Have you exercised regularly, particularly working on your bum? In the era of the ass, you should always take care of your knees

We finally caved in—if nothing else, we stopped with the hypocrisy. At least we are honest and now we love our big, fat, greedy asses openly, proudly, selfishly, unconditionally. If nothing else, we are not pretending anymore

We are free. We don't want to be anything else but what we are.
The problem is that thing that we are

The thing that I am

She fell asleep grumpily

The train—the rhythm of movement—light flickering

The train
She loved to travel on trains and to pretend that she was running to her office

She works in a restaurant

She hates her job, but the weakness passes quickly when she remembers about money
She remembers about money and starts scraping the dishes with even more energy

(Motivational letter. Fuck off.
System—the self-deluded rapist, who believes he is gentle. And not only is forceful, but demands reciprocity, demands from us to be motivated, inspired by him. He demands love)
He was coming to that restaurant very often, on his lunch break. He caught one of the girls washing the dishes, looking at him like from a portal to another dimension
Real people with real jobs and strong hands, he thought, watching her scrubbing the greasy trays
They are strong
They eat well
He went hard

He decided at that moment he would try to think less about sex
He left a generous tip
Later after work, he saw the same woman drinking at a nearby bar alone
She looked tired, pale and not so strong as she seemed in the restaurant, even fragile
They chatted a bit; with immigrants he talked about immigrant issues; it is irresistible—
This is at least the third time that bodies of immigrants have fallen from an aircraft in this area—have you read the newspaper? How did they get inside the plane?

Someone must be incredibly desperate to leave their country in that way!

Yes, the falling bodies—she nodded her head and spread her legs a bit so she could touch his knee

I like your strong legs

I like your strong accent

They exchanged mobile numbers and the following evening they made the hotel arrangement

Now that is finished as well

He won't be coming to that restaurant anymore

Here: The Conspiracy of Quasi Temporality

It is true that places can be haunted not just by ghosts of the dead, but also by ghosts of the living
Who are just like those dead, unable to part from that particular space
They are floating with the moonlight, mesmerised like babies with soft animal cot mobiles
They grow with the grass
Limbs scattered with insects
Tangled in the curtains
Tripping over the chairs
They sing with the owls, howl with the dogs
The heart sunken into mattresses
Gliding through always the same streets
At the same time an integral part of that place and not present at all
Their time is just their time
Their time is some other time
Conscious absence
They are looking for an exit, or they do not let go:
That pleasure. That pain. That guilt. That sickness. That anger. That lover. That mother. That father. That shame. That summer. That point.

The living who are just like those dead left frozen in the endless now, in an event that is rewinding constantly, again and again, like a film cliché of a failed, but good, policeman, playing a video of his beautiful, happy but dead family.

(Dreams about high efficiency, expertise of a rebellious derelict. Because at the end of the day, we are all derelicts)

Their smiles next to the swimming pool: "C'mon, Daddy!"- little owl voices again and again. Hand entangled in her hair waving again and again. That truck coming again and again. Dead again and again. While the body is living by its own necessity of the flesh

We stayed in that house

Forever

Husbands all left. Couldn't cope with the tension. And now our children are leaving. One by one

Just us

Sisters

Our parents died

For some, that is the only way to get out of here

Here: the place that exists before the world
Here is protecting us from There

Our mother wouldn't let us go
Daughters: not to be touched by men
Always daughters, never wives
The children from the mountains, moved to the city—
And the city was shouting: Smelly peasants!
And the city was shouting: Go back where you came from!
And the city was shouting: I am so shiny, come and touch me!
And the city was shouting: Sexy tits!
And the city was shouting: Come and join us, run away from home!

And the city was shouting. And the city was shouting. And the city was shouting
I dyed my blonde hair to bright red. Our mother caught me, pushed me into the bathroom and scraped my skull with wire and washing powder. Rinsing and soaping. Rinsing and soaping
All day
Because. Because only sluts. Only sluts. Only sluts have hair like that

And our mother worked and sighed, worked and sighed. She could pick up nettles with her bare hands. Her hair was long and gray, and her legs were swollen blue landscapes—

A map of a big river delta, its bulging meanders—straining in nylon knee-high socks, in skin colour

When she was a girl, she was the best in her class. Finished all and only four years of her school with straight As

She wanted her children to be engineers

Summers were long. Children left on the mountains over the whole summer

Sometimes we were hungry. Sometimes we had to hunt. The sunlight, the clouds. Tasteless black birds. Bitter mushrooms. Sweet roots. The world and its rules as seen in photographs on the pages of shiny magazines. The city was shouting, and we were putting our makeup on, dreaming, always dreaming

We never left the dream, we never left

The garden and the trees and the corridors

I broke all my bones and now I am here. Now that is all over. I am here. Here is comfortable. Now everybody looks good

They did best they could
There was only one family and we were the only children. Our own families could not compete ever—they scrambled into unreal
And now that everybody is gone, we are children again, and our mother and our father

the proud owners of a new car (the first one in the street!) are still here in every brick they built
Admiration for every brick that was placed into those walls by bare hands of our mother and our father
Admiration for those walls
Our
Their walls

And You Shine Content

The city started to shrink, to tighten like a lasso around its own spindle

The first sign of that narrowing was the sudden appearance of people in military uniforms, scrappy, impaired

One Two Three Four

Until many tentacles of this of this dead, olive-coloured animal were darting all over the streets, filling the space, hunting us down in the space behind blinds, in the space between our four walls

Even a local lunatic was imitating the trend: walking up and down the street in a fake uniform

Before he was always in a rough woollen jumper that smelled of cooking

His name was

"The one who loves his fellow countrymen"

A bomb fell through the roof of his shabby home, and went twenty meters under the floor of his bedroom

Didn't explode

They lived

The smelliest house around was the only house that was hit, and now it was surrounded with yellow tape with skull emoticons:
Danger! Danger! Avoid!

The neighbours secretly thought that somebody should have put up that tape even before the bomb fell, but they didn't say anything
Now he replaced his woolen jumper with t
he uniform
And his street preaching—
YOUR DAYS ARE NUMBERED AND YOU ARE ON THE WRONG SIDE!
YOUR SIDE IS WRONG!
With aggressive shouting, calling out remarks as much packed with anger
(TWATS, JOIN THE FIGHTERS ON THE FRONT LINES! YOU DIRT!)
As the queues in front of the embassies were dense with all of those who wanted to leave
(If it is the last thing we ever do!)
As much as the public transport was bursting with people— human flesh, squeezed into a rectangle of red-hot metal buses

(She felt a stranger press her behind with his pelvis, strongly
In this crowd, it is hard to tell who is doing what on purpose or is just forced to grip next to the closest body like one sardine to another
She is wearing something green, he thinks she is doing the same thing as he is; he nods to her full of respect (for the olive green); she nods back, imitating a facial expression she doesn't understand in full: Who-Knows-He-Might-Have-A-Gun)

The television was announcing that all was going as planned, excitedly emitting video postcards from just across the border of crippled corpses thrown onto each other: a mother on a father on a neighbour on a son on a daughter—making together an interactive organic sculpture that celebrated the victory

(Switch the channel!)

The scenery was made of streets edged with chewed-by-bullets buildings, like alien termite colonies, or like a lace tablecloth spread for the feast of ravenous gods, enjoying the delicacy of hunted-down game

(Just switch the channel!)

The border was an obsessive idea: parents trashing maps, drawing new imaginary borders in the air

Drunk

Discontinued

Unusable parents

Foraging through wild pop-up flea markets—

A long line of distorted cardboard boxes, stretching for miles, on which people were selling toilet paper. Powdered milk, canned fish. Prescription drugs, without a prescription. Family jewels. Old fur coats smelling of lavender and sour cabbage rolls

Object invasion, objects that are reproducing, flooding, attacking and devouring time and meaning

Like a small child amazed by its surroundings. Like a small child that knows every leaf shape and every ant trail in their garden, that is how she was aware of streets and faces
We are all on the streets, everything is on the streets

There is no privacy in a war

(Here they are, the divine creatures, how beautiful she looks, and that dress of hers!
And that boy of hers! His parents work abroad, he lives alone, they send money, he sniffs glue: I saw seven of me, with seven keys for seven doors to seven hells or seven heavens)

She was 15. And it was completely obvious to her. Impossibly boring. And totally unbearable.
The movement of organic processes

Untransparent, unstoppable

She hates her new breasts, her belly, her heavy arms, the stretch marks, hers
The widest thighs in the world
The large mahogany wardrobe in her parents' bedroom, handles—the metal eyes that are watching her
Nightmares in sweaty children's heads
(There is always somebody who has seen everything)
She opens the doors and dives into her mother's clothes
Little girl sniffing her absent mother's clothes

(Soft)

Now she takes out a 2-for-1 box of chocolate cookies that somebody sent from somewhere, sits on the floor and eats

One by one

Does not chew

Faster she swallows

Thinks and forgets, forgets and thinks

Touching her thighs after each mouthful

(Consequences should be ignored)

Wrappers hiding in her pockets

(All evidence should be destroyed)

Breathing and swallowing. Calming pain of this gorge spreading

Penetration of organic matter into organic matter

She hates the body

(One day it will be perfect, just perfect!)
Closes the wardrobe. Throws up in the toilet

(All would be better without sound. Switch it off!)

The autumn was hot
The concrete was heating up, her thighs were her enemies—sticking to the plastic seats in buses

The sound of her skin flopping. Of her skin peeling of the plastic seat

(The city is a wet metal bucket over my head. Ding, dong!)

The moon was a rounded scarab with golden, vibrating wings

The moon was a golden pebble

(That I swallow with the same dedication as I devour the chocolate from my mother's wardrobe)

Songs about carelessness and freedom: Out, out we will go!

Everything was just one big Now in which objects were piling up

("Decadence and excess at the end of the century," 20 years later fashion magazines will conclude, recommending warmly the style: it's this season's must-have)

And people were piling up, who were objects too and exploding in this meaty firework:
Dusty shoulder pads, diffuse way of walking, often in the middle of the road, half-empty plastic bags in their hands, fluttering in the wind, printed with big letters:

I (heart) my country

Nobody's beasties unpleasantly imposing intimacy, with their supple and suspicious eyes
(I wouldn't be surprised if they change into people during the full moon, not werewolves but weremen)

Boys/Men walking with legs wide apart

Freshly shaven heads

Girls/Women pressed into plastic clothes

(The moment you are a queen, under those lights on that dance floor)

Hair dyed into rusted iron

Lips bright red

(The old one, with scars all over her bare back, is laughing loudly with two soldiers while hanging in between their shoulders: Hey, I am not afraid of dicks! No fear of cocks, boys!)

Eyelashes coated in a thick layer of sticky mascara. The trembling tarantula limbs

(The daylight comes and... we don't want to go home)

There is something in the curves and in the firmness of all of those bodies that sings:

We have nothing but this body

And this body is a

Diamond

The pleasure of the shining

(You shine content)

 And no it's not easy to be this body

(The crystal lattice)

Tension

While the World Was Disappearing, We Grew and Grew

Look at that big one in white trousers: she is going to buy more bread. She is hungry, tired, she killed her third lover this week, she is hiding a pigeon in her shirt, or a black, long-haired guinea pig named Satan!

(Her legs are skinnier than mine)

And look at that fast man in the uniform! That is actually a woman dressed up as a guy, and she is in love with that big one. She is following her, she will get her, together they will go to the war and pick up stuff from abandoned houses. They will gather some money and will be happy in love—

Two girls sitting in a local park, skipping school again

Watching passersby, inventing stories about them

It seemed like the autumn leaves were falling down faster and more from the vibrations of their laughter

(First time I saw you on a train: coming back from The Science Museum. You were travelling with your parents.

You looked like the future

The way the future looks like in the posters communicating regeneration plans: cleaned, in new colours, almost achievable and yet not present

The parents' confusion at your bubble gum chewing with your mouth wide opened to the world,

was presenting even more, to the altar of voracious gods, their flaming golden baby)

And then a group of people entered the park with bags
Sacks
Blankets
Dogs
Children

"I can't stand these refugees, look what they are doing with this city!" - she said

(Her friend was a refugee, she came with her mother and brother, her father staying in a besieged hospital)

Their eyes met
The moment of understanding
Realisation in which her thoughts became just hers
The moment she will often remember with heaviness and shame
The breaking point
Before and after
She become much older, much bigger
She dived out from inside of herself:
No, I don't think that actually
Not me, I am just repeating what everybody is saying constantly

And they are repeating what is repeated

Yes, I know

I don't like "all this" either

Except for you and me

Like there is nobody

And I found you

(You glow at top of the school staircase)

I don't want to be here

And this wind

Here, the wind is constantly blowing!

There is something in this weak, ruthless wind; it plays with people's minds

Do you feel it?

It brings me memories I don't want to have

It brings me cards, each day, one card—

I think I learned how to read them. Today ten of diamonds drifted through the air to me, and that means money, baby!

We will get some money
She loved the way she was talking, there was something calm something motherly, magical about her

They were both fifteen
They were sitting in the park, hours passing
It was boring
It was always boring
Boring, boring, boring
It was ringing in her ears like a tottery tram, going from one shit-hole to another

From one suburb to another
Through corn and turnip fields
Soggy, naked ground
Everything is brown
If it is not concrete, it is brown
They went to a shop
They were stealing
They were stealing every day
Roasted hazelnuts, chocolate bars
Chewing gum
At the exit, security took them aside, demanding that they empty their pockets
The whole shop was screaming at the same time, waving their hands , threatening with the police:

You two are here every day! Shame on you!

You parents should have spanked you more often!

And you are girls?!

Why are you doing this?

We are refugees, we don't have any money
That was a half-truth

Something that she will perfect later in life; she will become an expert in half-truths

(Lie is an emotion, she thought. At least in her case

Lie is an emotion

lies revolve around somebody who is important, and

who needs to be protected from unnecessary information

although, very often, that somebody is

the very liar,

it is me!

The objectivity is drawn from the survival laws

of a human heart in moments of weaknesses

and a true belief that waters strained in the meanders will return to the right flow

Gently

To lie is to create privacy, in the moments when a liar thinks that it is absolutely nobody's business what the liar does or how she lives—she is busy with herself and a lie secures a free space, free time—disconnecting the world from the liar's privacy, from the liar's "being alone"

Lie is a fantasy, a story, an art

A liar is flexible and understands much more realities from many
that are constantly stretching that word "truth" like old
       chewing gum scraped from the sole of
a tyrant's boot
Lie is an attempt to control (unpleasant) reality with words—the belief in the power of words
Magic believes the same
Abracadabra
Poetry as well
Religion: Let it be light, and there was light
Truth is without emotions and overrated. I was always truthfully telling you that I was a scumbag!

Truth is, very often, the last refuge of merciless, unscrupulous scumbags.
That was her final conclusion on that matter, and this—as long as death does not catch me in a lie.

Naked in death, unresolved accounts, wide open profiles on all social networks
(How can you live like that?) My laptops, phones, profiles, they will die before me.
If not, don't read! Believe in me! Believe in us! In the best possible version of us!
As I do believe in that, all the rest are dead ends, crumbs, attempts, all the rest is not important)

They let them go with a mixture of condemnation and pity
The longest steps took them back to the park

(Those long, aimless steps, throughout the last eternal days of childhood. A whistle through the narrow streets, wheels on a bike, lizards soaking up the sun)
Let's find some money!

They went in front of a nearby hotel to ask people, going in and out

Mostly men

(Because men have money)

For some change

Most of them wouldn't acknowledge them at all, like at the time, popular seer-healer, with a big diamond letter R on his lapel

He just slid away from them, almost not touching the ground
He had a show on the national TV

Her neighbor loved his show. She gave her last money for some miracle pig fat. Need will make you believe in anything. She gave her last money to buy herself the ability to look at her husband's needy, ever sinking eyes. He died after a month, leaving behind him three children and a bucket full of pinkish, stale pig fat

Then, a big, muscular guy in a leather jacket emerged from the dark

All sweaty, grinding his teeth, talking loudly

His arms were rowing through this continuous wind like he was chasing away all the spirits that were entering his nostrils, mouth, ears, scratching his freshly shaven cheeks:

"Hey you, women, kids, whatever! Where are you heading to? I am going to see my mum; you know, even I have a mother!"

"And she loves me madly!"

"Mothers are crazy!"
"You don't have money, ha? This uncle here has money,

dope, speed and a big boner! Joking! I have Coca-Cola! Want it? Why are you dressed up like that? Has somebody died? Why don't you put on some flowery miniskirts and stuff?"

He started to rummage through his pockets, throwing around crumpled betting tickets and pumpkin seed shells, muttering into his stiff chin:
"I am out of cash"
He looked left and right and showed the direction with his head:
"Follow me!"
The two of them executed the order like soldiers, and walked behind him to an off-licence
Resembling two big penguins

He whispered something to the owner, then smiled, so tense as
if his face was going to burst:
The boss says, take what you want!
If you need anything, you know where to find me—he winked
and staggered off across the street
They took a few beers and joined kids in front of the shop
The kids were drinking, smoking, asking for money and
listening to a young man, freshly back from the war:
We would empty the missiles and fill them with money, the
other side the same but with weed, and we would fire that
across the front lines
So we were smoking a lot

I wouldn't know if I killed somebody, you just fire a missile

I am sure I must have

Then the boys started talking about army recruitment and
what were the best ways to avoid it: Just say that you are mad
or a junkie or a gay

The best is to hide

Then some of them started to argue that all of them should go
to the war and help their country

At that moment, she drifted away—

Observing her forehead—it was shiny, big, rounded, china
moon-like

She put her head on her shoulder

The cans were empty

What shall we do tomorrow?

I don't know

Depends what the wind will bring

Probably, nothing again—their laughter—metal coins falling on a pavement, ringing through the hollow night

She touched her face

They were kissing long
While the world was disappearing, her lips were soft

While the world was disappearing, we grew

And grew

Until Such Time
Reality Is Just an Abstraction

I t is always like that when entering a club

The sense of importance mixed with the feeling that you are at the mercy of snipers

Of those who are already there

Newcomers vs indigenes

Across the dance floor, she swings her angles

This angular beauty, her rapturous angles

Femininely carrying her male connotations

And then sticks her bare back on the sweaty walls written and rewritten and written again:

Long live the bride! The bride—The bride goes to your school! The bride is pregnant

Death to faggots. Crossed-out faggots. Added: violence, death to violence. Crossed-out violence.

Added: Muslims, Gypsies, Catholics, sluts. Death to Muslims, Gypsies, Catholics, sluts. Crossed-out Muslims, Gypsies, Catholics, sluts. Added: everybody

Death to everybody!

Equality!

Sketch of mental process of reaching collective correctness

Maturation–Masturbation

Maturation through masturbation

Fight the bully. We are all a bully when we can be one

Then it is not your fault, of course not
Sometimes life is calm and happy
That leopard coat and plastic sunglasses
Anyway, weddings are just "something for girls"

I dance I break the air, I break the habits of my arms
I break habits of my legs, I break the stiffness that all the eyes
on me cause, I break the space between me and her, I break
myself
I dance
I want to leave

Eyes are everywhere

Keen interest or a sneer, heaven and hell of practicing mating
customs of night birds. The ones who were already giving head
and the ones who will be giving head soon
The beauty without strength and peace, porous, letting in
auras and wills of others, of the kind they pity while
ravenously chewing on it

[the feeling of guilt
sewed tightly in
the school girl's skirt lining

still learning (her) mother tongue

(long, gentle licking) in aspic

In thin slices

forgotten in the fridge

stains in greasy eyes

polished hard (in boys' toilets) winged beetles

shiny buttons on the musty, wrinkled blouse for school]

She was admiring her on her natural ability to dance. She never knew what to do with her arms. Not even while she was walking. She was always aware of the disharmony of her steps and her arms

Always aware

Of each limb separately and of every stiff move

Just to be her! Just to be free!

Riding the light carousel in the woollen discotheque, tucked in and safe from the outside world

She left the friend to squeeze next to a guy on the dance floor and went outside

Even now, very drunk, she was aware of each step

(I am walking like a windup duck)
The landscape was going up and down like a yo-yo.

It wasn't better, not even with her eyes closed, the same image,

the same trembling
Throwing up in a corner
The silver moon on a spring
Up and down
Up and down, under the night crooked shadows of the estate buildings
The tram station under oily night sky hanging heavily onto the naked tree-claws
The avenue
Rolling uncompromisingly into the event horizon
(What happens to particles in the past is only decided when they are observed in the future, until such time—reality is just an abstraction)
The dry prairie sanding the bones. Some of them will be found, dug out—it is fascinating how it is possible to identify human remains, from just a fraction of a bone—that is all we are, organic matter plus information, the information lingers a while after us
The rest will continue to sink into the deeper layers of history, soft sand, oblivion
Unfound and missing
Fossils strained under the heavy
Salty, open sea.
She was a thirsty child, in the distance the far away light of a tram that will take you to the safety

(the trucks sounding just like ships—that is always when a horn beeps, she imagines an ocean cruiser, and doesn't think much about it,
doesn't ask questions just simply as that: just a few blocks away, here in this deep continent a ship is passing by)

Instead of leaves on the branches of trees black birds are growing—taking off and landing

Flying—Pushing—Squawking:

Alive black treetops falling apart and gathering again

Shaping and reshaping

Breathing in and breathing out

Down to the pavement—feathers and baby chicks

People were waiting for the tram under those wings, watching out for the bird's excretions

Her focus from the shapeshifting treetops was soon moved towards somebody's intense presence-

Few meters down the street a man was standing

A stiff watcher

She knew him he was always waiting for the tram at the same stop, at the same time as she did. She pretended she didn't see him. (If I don't see you, you don't exist)

They got on the same tram

They got off at the same stop

She speeded up and could feel the waves of his huge stomach. IIc was fast, he would catch her
He grabbed her arm and turned her towards him

His breath of onions and barbeque:
I see you were celebrating tonight, lots of drinking? Boys and stuff? Come with me!
We will have good times, I have whisky!
Don't pretend now! I saw how you were watching me every night:
You watch me and I watch you

I know you are young and shy, but you will get over it
C'mon, C'mon
Tight hugs, humid, hairy hands
Imprisoned with his body
She struggled, he was stronger
Scratching her with his beard all over her neck and face, her elbows were falling into his jelly-like belly
But she was faster
The man—The girl—The trance—The confusion—The feathers—The clouds—The dust—The seized opportunity—To slip—And to take off
She managed to use the moment of his incautiousness to wriggle out from his squeeze and to kick him in his balls
Surprised, he let his arms hang next to his body—Quiet, slippery, two dead fish
She started to run.
She was running like she had never run before, while he was crying behind her back, in an almost inhuman voice

Like one of the croaking birds

Like a man

Like a woman

Like a tabby

Like a baby

Like the loneliest creature in the universe

She was losing her breath, running fast and feeling slightly sorry for this materialised loneliness and its weeping:

Come back I love you! Nobody will love you like I do! Come back!

She didn't stop running

It was already dawn

The Doll's Game

She noticed as a child that grownups were not listening
That they were not listening when they should have been listening and that they were listening when they shouldn't have been listening:
Her
When she was playing with her dolls
Her
Giving the voice to the unmoving
Silent lips
To the secret life of those dolls
The life, not always happy life
The adults were listening and giggling:
Isn't she sweet, such an imaginative child! Bit gloomy. Will you be an artist when you grow up?
Then she surely needs a rich husband!
She went quieter and quieter, until she discovered that she didn't need to speak out loud, that dolls' stories can flow in her head, without any sound, nobody could hear her thoughts, and in those stories
Without fighting

She was free

To build herself inside of herself

You Should Show that Love Sometimes

First you would hear the
Metal garden gates
A loud bang
And then her high heels
Smashing the concrete
With the power of a CEO
Causing a tight mixture
Of anticipation, anxiety and a weird feeling of guilt
For no obvious reason—
Mummy is home
With suitcases full of sweets for children and nicely packed stories for grownups
Mothers
Oh, those mothers
Oh, mothers mothers
Tough blondes in charge
Of surface mining
Of men digging—He is alive, he is well

He is inside. Earning, producing—

Mothers not interested in children

Producing children

Spreading clean sheets

Serving food

Laying on entertainment

There was no entertainment

No, no entertainment

Once she was offered a house in a holy land. She refused it. She didn't want to live there. She said it was too flat and there were no birds

A flat pancake—your holy land

No not for me, sir

She also said that in some countries, where she was on her business trips, there were no cotton pants

You had to wait for your turn to buy them

With your bare bottom? Children would ask, chuckling

And that in another place, women had the longest legs she had ever seen, and they were drinking like it was an award-winning activity

smashing their long, bony knees on old, cobbled streets

She tried eels and frogs and snakes and jelly-like desserts
Drank Martinis and Black Russians and White Russians
And flew in airplanes where lunches were nicely packed in a plastic tray
(She would always bring little satchels of sugar and salt and plastic cutlery with the logo of the airline home)
And was followed in some places by an agent who would tell her if she
Had gone too far
You always have to go too far—to understand the cold drinks

from the cold war brown drink cabinets
We all went too far
That morning on her 37th birthday, she looked at herself in the mirror
And finally understood that weird expression on her mother's face she noticed as a child:
She observed her from her window—
She was thin
Always looking like a girl from a faraway
Good bone structure, talent hunters would say
Now in her memory, it was always sunset

Roof tops and tree tops

Sinking slowly into the sticky apricot sunset jam

Everything was just floating there

And her mother floating there too

Weightless

Smoking

Smoking like those cowboys on horses riding off into the horizon, smoking like those French stars in their convertibles, curving

Above the Mediterranean

Smoking like a free woman lingering in a bar, ready for some new loving

Like a secret agent

Like Bond, James Bond

That was how she looked to her

Puffing those hours and hours away

Floating in warm sunsets

But her weird expression was always a mystery until that morning when she saw her own face in the mirror: swollen eyes, endless boredom
Yes, that's it!

Her mother was bored
And that was a special kind of elaborate boredom
Boredom of a factory worker who decided he would stay forever in a factory he didn't like
Who decided that every day would be the same and not quite satisfactory, but that every day would be familiar and that was good enough. Not the boredom one feels when there is nothing to do.
This was boredom where
Everything was boring
The very essence of her Universe was boring
This apricot sunset—just materialised reassuring boredom
She understood her mother's face now
And she loved her more than ever

Around the place where she was smoking
A circle of cigarette buds was spreading like
An upside down halo
Like a little stage
Waiting for her to come back
And conduct yet another
Magnificent sunset of thrills

This Is the Colour of Happiness

She lived with her mother in a house with the garden next to a wood

They were watching TV all day and all night

(Latin tears under the dishevelled palm trees)

They were making bread from the greyish flour they got from a humanitarian help, in big bags

Her father was reported missing. Her mother reported him missing. Just for the sake of it: to make a point

They weren't worried

They didn't believe he was really missing

He wasn't missing

He just made the best of the chaotic times

He had a heavy presence—

(Her father did not approve her tree climbing skills—

Yes, that is right, just show to everybody how manly you are!

His fat guest was grinning, holding his beer

He stamped on her roller skate and then kicked it, laughing and staggering
Her father was laughing and staggering as well

That staggering was weakness
That laughter was weakness
She jumped down from the tree to the grass and was standing still
Monumental
Like a concrete sculpture celebrating victory over fascism
Watching them leaving the garden—that was the last time she saw him. Don't be surprised if you find out later in life that you have half-brothers and half-sisters —her mother told her. She was imagining her half-brothers and half-sisters like perfect beings of light. She wanted them to find her. She would be better with them)

She felt easier after he left. She felt guilty about that. She did miss him
Surrounded by wallpapers with lighter square patches at the places where photos were taken off the wall
Mostly photos of her father
They were eating bread in the orange room, snuggled up next to each other under the blanket. The light of the setting sun entering through the half-opened blinds, Latin American soaps on TV, one after the other, and one warm bun after the other. At moments, it looked as if there were a big mirror there instead of the TV, reflecting the slow motion of golden dust falling all over them and the objects, reflecting two rounded faces the colour of pomegranate—
The sun was King Midas and everything that its ray fingers touched would be fossilised into gold

When her father was painting the room in orange, he said: "This is the colour of happiness."

Shadows of the outside world were sneaking through the

window, getting longer, sliding across the walls, their two faces, the furniture, those long slow shadows were the only proof that they were running out of time

Covered in breadcrumbs, not moving her eyes from the screen, her mother said, yawning:

"This would be a good moment for a big meteor to hit and burn everything down—to finish with all this

With this rude existence"

The Past Is a Grotesque Animal*

(*Title of a song by the band Of Montreal)

She never knew if what happened was for real
She wasn't sure if she should talk about it—Maybe I invented everything—Auto-fiction
(Bravo! Sit down, straight A from your personal mythology)

Everything is just an overload of images. No context, no continuity.
History is exactly that—an overload of images to which we are trying to give a meaning

The difference between a collector and a hoarder—I am a hoarder
I am hoarding images, memories
Bulking them one on the top of the other, leaving them to the moths, rats and rot, deformed, maltreated, used
Needed
"Micro-abused child" – she told that to just one person, once, in a joke. And never again to anybody else
Micro abusing
Micro self-abusing—Scratching your cuticles until you bleed

The Future Is an Animal Dancing in a Coffee Cup

You can see the future from a coffee cup, if you have the gift - her mother would say, rotating her cup to mix well the thick coffee residue

If you have it, you will see the shapes dancing and writing out a story about you!

I can see hearts: Empty hearts. Heavy hearts. And the most important:

The reversed heart

The one that has seen it all and it's still there full of love, but

Twisted. Twisted love

I can see male figures and female figures, entangled into a ball of causes and consequences rolling down the branching roads, disappearing more and more into the unrelatedness

And now you can make a wish

Spin the cup and stab the residue with your finger. Go on! Everybody has wishes!

What kind of a person are you

If you don't have any wishes?

Freedom Throws the Prescribed Tomorrow Down the Mountain

The smell of autumn leaves—
Decomposing, melting

Walnuts and pears—
Ripening, falling

Smoke—
Branches, plastic, it is burning
Coal, wood sold by meter—
It is here, we have it, it is good

The birds are flying back to the South—
Constellations are gliding

Her mother came back from the mountain, smelling of wet wool, of animals and herbs
She brought a story of a woman, that lived there, not so long ago—
She threw 11 of her newborn children down the cliff—
They said, they were counting
She had many lovers—
They said they were watching

She wanted to keep it a secret—

They said they were sure of it

(I can hear them breathing through the walls

They have shiny teeth, sharp eyes)

But her mother thought that she simply didn't want to have any more children

Sleeping with your husband was just another obligation to go through during the day

And now that forest is haunted by the ghosts of her children. And everybody knows that unchristened, dead children turn into noisy forest demons

A man killed a wild boar, an alpha male, that belonged to the forest—and that which belongs to the forest, that is forbidden. The demons got angry

Now, just two months after the kill, the hunter is dying of a fast-developing cancer

His body is turning into wild meat

Untamed

Uncontrollable meat

His body turning into a demon that devoured him at the end
And of course, it was a woman's fault. A dead woman's fault, that is

Everybody knows that women turn men's bodies into wild, uncontrollable meat

They found his freezer bleeding with boar's blood, there was an unexplained power cut
The wild rotting blood was spreading on the carpet, smelling sweet and sickly—like a baby

Nobody tasted not a bite of that game

It is that time of the year, the month of slaughtering domestic animals.
The animals are always given the same name.
New animal, old name
The name lives, the animal dies
Every year, every moment, the mechanism is replacing its parts. Everywhere is the same.
Only there, this is rather more obvious
It is very beautiful there now, clear, no fog, the sunshine is everywhere, and blackberry bushes are deep red

Chimneys
Warm lights in windows
Sticky air, let's stick together
Family
It never stops
Family
You are my family

It never stops

Animals

It never stops

You are my animals
It never stops

If Only You Could Have Seen Those Divine Herons

(In memory of E.)

Weak, transparent wind. Skin. The body is getting colder. Skin. The will is getting colder
The streets are, the thoughts are unfolding down the hills, towards the rivers, towards the low Sun
The unstable trees, the wind—flags and fanfare under the yellow griffin's stiffened wings
Towards the point where swells this big water, scratched by rusty barges
The wind, old wind
The daydream cut with sudden fear: nothing will ever happen.
I will stay right here forever, at this point where the wilderness is growing over concrete spaces, and the concrete is just a thin veneer
Temporary domesticated quicksand
At this point where swells this big water disturbed by birds, by the thought that it is somehow easier to go away if there is water
Disturbed by the fact that there is no forever
Cold not fresh wind manipulates
Forcing the movement:
She threw on a cardigan, hanging on the chair: sharp pain

A sewing needle her mother left in the pocket pricked her finger—

Sleeping beauty and the poisonous prick, to find any love in her heart—that was the trick—she said

Deep red spot, quickly grew, and started to run, dripping at the
open newspaper on the table, the miniature squashed
rosebuds of her blood framed one photo in the obituary page

There are no stories about the dead—

How they lived? Were they happy? Favourite colour? Favourite
food? The best summer?

Just black and white photos: You will be missed.

And dead sentences. You will be missed.

Just pages and pages filled with faces staring at you

Will I be missed?

Most of them the first and the last time featured in the press.
Pages that housewives use to wrap jars of homemade jam
so they don't break in transport, when taking them to their
grown-up children

Or to start a fire

A familiar disinterest was radiating from those narrow una-
voidable eyes: No, not disinterest, it was a focus

Deep focus

(Shiny movements in the beasts' night eyes, focused and
waiting for The End. Passionate about the end)

Pinning inside a foreign object, a crushed metal, a fist
squeezing a piece of paper in a coat pocket

(I will, just watch me)
The reversed heart. Bleeding cuticles

She couldn't stop following the clear line of that long neck
Tense nostrils—never tamed
Little doily collar made her look even more unreal—
Like she was made in a factory by bored but efficient workers
Imprinting their bored, overworked souls and skills of their fingers into her features
The image of beauty of no longer existing (some)body
Memory of light
That face was a wave and she was a surfer
A big surf wave rolling and lifting, her body hair erected
She put her blood-covered finger in between her legs
The excitement wouldn't stop
(That could almost be my own memory—A photo taken at the end of the school. It will stay forever in the glass vitrine in my parents' house. In the past, you are yet to become. In a wavering, water sculpture of auto-fiction. A highway through the dancing sand—The granulated photo content
The warm lips and
The cold lips

Painlessly crushed

On the edge of two-dimensionality)

Without touching

There is no place of meeting but

I know you too well

She tore the photo from the newspaper and put it into her diary

Dear diary, I became obsessed

I want I need

To be obsessed

Dear diary...

That is when I first saw your mother

*

You came to the story, if there was a story, a bit later—an image to rule them all

An unaware narrator, unreliable narrator

A scarab rolling the undefined matter into a finely rounded dream

Up the chimneys—Up the streets—Up the hills—Up the stratosphere—Up—Up and Up

Away from the world

You should have seen that divine heron on the greasy pavement in front of the kebab shop!
There he is, Akhenaten!—I could hear sighs through the corridors of the hospital
There he was—like his mother made by the same factory workers, but this time something happened
Maybe it was a sunny day, or the syndicate sent halved animals, pigs or cows, to everybody for free, to keep families fed and calm
This time there was something soft, something gentle in their creation—a sketch of a promise, a promise

*

In the opposite direction and down
Down through unclear tunnels

Down through velvet layers
I was stalking you
Dear diary
All the way to the clean crisp sheets in your mother's house.
To the rattling of the coffee cups that you hear in your shallow sleep and to the free radio that announces the news as if the world exists
I was stalking you through this city and
This city was a surrender

(A city is persistent desire for another city)

This city was everything, its borders fading into endless now—
banality sticky with pebbles and sparkles

My desire erected and proud sticking out, impossible to hide

You saw me and you took me home

Your hands are the hands of a woman. The way you hold your cigarette

We were hiding in your dark house while days were arriving slowly and uncompromisingly

My family didn't talk to me, I was with a man

You were feeding me. I was becoming big and soft. Unmovable

The bronze bust of your mother made by your artist father was sniffing us from above—

And how did she die?

She killed herself

I wanted to know all. The things even you could not

possibly know

I wanted to solve her death

As if death can be solved

As if she still existed. Now, not in a form of a human being. But in a form of a dialogue, between me and you. Between me and me. Between me and the universe

*

I was observing you for hours. I loved watching you pacing around the room
You were talking to yourself chasing dragons and ghosts
Half-naked, in jeans. Your narrow hips. I was daydreaming in the smoking haze—
You were one of the street boys leaning on hot walls in vivid colours somewhere faraway
(The non-existing faraway)
Where palm trees were growing and big, salty waves were washing the roads.
Yes, you were that street boy. On the streets of freedom
In the avenues of that Utopia people were carrying automatic guns and drinking cold beer. There under those palm trees. And children were carrying guns and wrinkled smiles. The sea was shimmering and tropical birds flying over. People were catching them and then they would look after them
There, people loved their birds
We were there to remain, in love with everything that was not there, in love with absence

*

You are your mother. I am wearing her jewelry.

I am dressing you up in your dead mother's clothes

I am putting her lipstick on your big lips
You are watching yourself in the mirror smiling with that wrinkled smile, stroking your hips.
Your legs!

Not a woman anywhere with better legs than yours! I am jealous. You are prettier than me

"I am prettier than you"—you are looking yourself in the mirror, fascinated

I am lifting your skirt. I adore your legs. My first orgasm with a man

A rare one

Dear diary,

They are so rare that I am writing them down

Like making an almanac of animals at the verge of extinction

*

Us, young bodies

And borders

Closed

Us, soft bodies

And aggression

Rising

Us, gentle bodies

And death

Arousing

Us, our bodies

Curled up next to each other—Tight

Only then everything was alright

We are sleeping till late. We are sleeping till the evening. We are mostly sleeping
You wake often; we talk often, in pauses in between
two dreams.
I can hear the world behind the blinds. I can feel it penetrating the walls of desired cold

*

We are waking up often and you are telling me the stories about your mother:
Her grandfather was a spy. He knew fluently 5 languages and lived in 5 different countries, and everybody thought he was a baker
He was killed in the battle for Stalingrad
And that bullet not only brought him his death—but pursued his family—over the whole century
His mother told him that his grandmother saw men hanging, in their family garden
Their legs twitching in the air
Above the endless muddy prairie
Men lingering. Twitching. They last in her memory. They are not passing. Twitching. Elevated towards the sun

She forgot who were those people—uncles, brothers, fathers.
She forgot what her mother told her but she remembered her
telling her that was the day that she took a gun and joined
the partisans

And she remembers the story how she escaped from a
concentration camp, and how she was running through a
forest while bullets were cutting her long hair

The sound of the bullets cutting her hair

She was brave and smart. From a fight to a fight she was getting
closer to one of the commandeers

A partisan star

They became a partisan power couple, and on the happiest day
of the war at a small, civil ceremony, they became the basic
unit of society

Love and ideas of equality, freedom, the rule of the people,
passion for the future and off course their youth were enough
to win

So, they won

*

The days are melting into the years amongst books, photos
and memories that are not even yours

But with a guilt that is only yours

The paradise of the revolution. The stars of the revolution.
The parasites of the revolution

The people, the streets, the uproar, flags and billboards, witty

slogans, the police, the tanks, the thrill—
The power

Fantasies about power uplift

Sharpen the glow in your eyes
After all my great grandfather, after all my grandfather, after
all my grandmother, after all my mother... After all. After all
The lukewarm everydayness
After all
You were interrupting our phone conversations shouting
at your imaginary spies: YOU IMBECILES!! YOU THINK I
DON'T KNOW YOU ARE FOLLOWING ME!? HERE I WILL
SAVE YOUR TIME: I HAD A BANANA FOR BREAKFAST IN
CASE YOU MISSED IT!!

*

Soon after the war they got a baby girl. The drug supplies were
poor and sporadic, and when the baby got meningitis, there
wasn't much they could do
But she wasn't giving up on her daughter that easily
She was rubbing her baby's limp, unresponding body with
herbs and brandy. Until the sun came up. Massaging those
small arms and legs. Until the moon came up. And wiping and
kissing her cheeks.
Until she rubbed the life back into her
The girl lived. But there were consequences. She stayed a child
all her 40 years of life. She died in a care home for people with
special needs
Two years after the first one they got another daughter, she was
unusually beautiful and resilient
From the beginning of the peace, her and her husband had
been constantly imprisoned by the new partisan government

Because of that bullet

They were representing a different left option and they were spending long periods on a naked rocky island—the prison for political enemies

The first they made you do is to hit the one who is closest to your heart

If it is your twin brother or sister, you will first hit them

Everybody was guilty

Everybody was quiet

The girls were looked after by their granny, whose heart closed that day when she saw her brothers hanging in the family garden

*

I remember frequent hospital visits—I was running through,

entangled in, fingers of fog that sprawl in the concrete hospital yard, and dissolve in the autumn sky

I am always entangled, I am always late

You are waiting for me

In your pajamas, delirious and beautiful, I am stroking your face
Letting its shape become real in my palm

Like a delicate bird in my palm, your face

The bird, sings -
How people are generally forgetting things!
I don't remember the reminder not to mention

Common places, the world powers
And not to implement that warm and friendly patriotism,
on which at the moment everybody has a hard on
The bullies from the war are the winners of the transition
And women, women are also the winners of the transition
according to the latest research—Something about flexibility
(Probably they think that they are enduring well, working long
shifts in nappies, without toilet breaks)
Hey what do they know
The rehabilitation of shit, that is what is going on at
the moment
Not even a real shit but some weakened shit
Like a homeopathic solution, patriotism diluted until it is safe
to use, still sticky enough to glue, where gluing is needed but
acceptable, politically correct—
Modern, justified—enriching the dull corporate globalisation.
Entertains. Decorates with some local colours and tastes
"Authentic flavours and colours"—get them along with your "I
am protesting," "This is all a conspiracy," "Shortcut to your
most spiritual spirituality," and "I am kinky" starter-pack

Even our perversions are now nicely packed with a price tag
and expiry date—

The system is safe

The system is stable

The wilderness is under control

I don't care, I am zero nationality, nationality neutral—a man
from the land in between

Anyway, it is another thing that he was hallucinating, that he
was a spy. I mean he was under the influence for a very long
time, and even now he is on prescription drugs. He has had an
implant sewn in, under his skin that supposed to block his

only passion

Passions are hard to block. Wilderness is hard to block

"The pervert found his object, that is his problem"

Replacement

It works for a while

And then everything explodes from the desire for the
real thing

Believe me I know

Sorry, I know you know, you were watching me for years

He was digging it up, with his fingers from under his skin,
so he

can shoot himself again

You can't understand how much he fucked up the company,
that fucked up all its clients—It was almost the most subversive
act of art I have ever seen. The site-specific virtuous
performance—

The artist is present and is fucking up the corporation!
The secret is not people like us all around the world
The secret is money. Give me all that money and I will take
down any government! Money is the best diplomacy
Yes, I know, good old excuse: no money, no anything else
But let me have at least something—an excuse
We were so stupid, so naive, the world will save us! But look at
the world! Who will save the world!
The fools did something unforgivable: they gave away the
names of activists along with the information

It is not about a recognition; it's jeopardizing the sources. They always give you away.
Never trust a cop or a politician

*

The old women were complaining about the draught.
Burly nurses dressed them up like little girls in flowery nightgowns and fluffy slippers, tucked them in blankets, and closed all the windows
But the galloping on the plush horse through the corridors of the hospital and around old women's dandelion heads didn't stop:

Ghosts of lonely children were looking for something soft

*

Your mother is in jail. Your father is in jail. Your mother is in jail. Your father is in jail
You are ugly and you are stupid

Children in school were barking at her, supported by politically ambitious teachers and parents

Back at home she lived with constant absence of her mother and father.

With time things started to settle a bit. They would imprison them only during state holidays and during visits of important foreign diplomats

Just in case

Her father became demented from all the blows he received in his head during imprisonment years

And her mother obsessed with bringing the truth on the day light, joining groups fighting to bring back the human rights to former political prisoners

She didn't have time to look after her demented husband and her daughter, so she put them both in institutions, but she didn't miss a single weekend—to visit them, and bring them a chicken soup

She believed in chicken soup

At the end her father didn't know who he was or where he was

He didn't die sad

He died on a rocking chair watching a pile of rubbish, from his hospital terrace, somewhere at the ugly outskirts of an ugly provincial town, thinking he was in Cuba—American, Russian, he didn't care

All he could see was a magnificent glistening sea

And giant, shiny silver fish jumping from the waves and disappearing into iridescent, turquoise waters

He would shout, from his terrace about what he could see:

MAGICAL JEWEL! THAT WAVE AND THE FISH! THE MAGICAL JEWEL! IN MY EYES THE MAGICAL JEWEL! HER HAIR IN MY HANDS IS TURNING INTO GOLDEN AND CRISP SEAWEED!

And nobody told him it was just a pile of rubbish, that is how he died

*

I left, but you never stopped to write to me about your revolutionary days, your mother and your auto-fictional enemies and comrades—
"Btw we all loved him... especially when he was a guest on the national TV and he was unable to speak. He is not the only one that used his background in advertising (he is even a poet):

Can you imagine all those crazed men of power willing to pay all that money to the little monkey that beats his bongo drums?
I mean OK you are not a monkey at all but a special kind of a person is needed for that. You have to act.

I have to act

All what people are doing normally—I have to act. You have to have a stamina for that. A backbone.
Not to allow not the tiniest tic. Yes you need to have a face for that, a poker face, or a smile from a commercial.
What do you think, why he took all those drugs?
He is like those girls in front of my building that are sucking Russian, Bulgarian, Romanian, Turkish... Name it, truck drivers' dicks. They are always high. Night and day. Ordinary girls, somebody's daughters, mothers... Overdoses, bodily fluids, diseases... I don't want to sound now like Charles Dickens...
Anyway, this guy was doing the same but for much bigger earnings.

Bigger earnings, bigger cocks
But there are no good guys! We are all bad guys!

IT'S NOT US
IT'S NOT THE PEOPLE
IT'S NOT THE PEOPLE
WHO IS IT, THEN??

Come down we are all here to help you

WHO IS THAT ALL?

Look around you: All those people.
All people are good people in their core and they want to help you
We all want to help you
The narrative lost its sense. You are talking stunned by fumes of your phantasmagoric revolution.
A prophetess that predicts the past.
You became several different persons
You are not in touch only when you are the worst of them—
the one whose eyes are not echoing,
Focused on The End

Passionate about "The End"

*

She went to study archaeology
Digging out the remains of ancient communications—she thought—

All stories are our stories

The university was boring, she couldn't attach to anything
It looked to her as if she would lose the world if she went into a narrow specialisation, but at the same time the world was un-reachable—She was just lingering in this in-between land, undefined and unrooted

She wasn't putting in effort

The only things she was fascinated with were lachrymatory Bottles : antique tear-catchers

She started to collect them
At one exhibition she met a young, promising artist, who was orphaned by the war
He came from mountains, and stone was something that he always loved.
He became one of the best sculptors in the country
They were seeing each other for some time

Once a week

Usually on Sunday

Soon they were married

He was joking that everybody knew something that he didn't—it looked like the state was giving homes to everyone for free, just he was always below on the list

He was advised to connect better; he didn't want to complicate things; he didn't want connections.

He just wanted a flat
Somewhere to live

So he worked hard and managed to buy a small flat
She was drinking
And collecting lachrymatory bottles
He was shaped and reshaped in the strict educational structure
Without parents to kiss and forgive small naughtiness
He was obedient
(Even in his death, he wanted to do a right thing. He died from a heart attack—his big gentle heart exploded, during his son's last hospitalisation. Like he wanted to do things in the right order, to die before his son, because no parent should outlive his children. His son died a month after him, without knowing his father was dead.)

He was obedient, but
He was strong

One of the people who were building the new world. New bridges. New roads. For free. Completely for free. He worked and he smiled. Worked and loved. He: the sparkly afterglow of the Revolution.

But she, she would sometimes think that he was a good person just because he never had the balls to be bad
He was never allowed to be bad

And all she wanted, sometimes

Maybe always

All she wanted now was to be bad

*

They say that she wasn't drinking during the pregnancy. She gave birth to a healthy boy. There is a photo in which she is struggling to hold her enormous baby

She was somehow smaller than that big baby boy

(She dreamt that her mother came to help her around that gigantic baby
She brought a chicken soup in a glass jar
Pieces of chicken
A wing
A leg
A crest
Pressed into the jar and covered in a clear yellow liquid like formaldehyde exhibits in a museum of mutants
Her mother's face
Under the partisan cap

Unnatural melted features—stretching sideways. Bony hands. Very warm hands. Radiating the heat.
Those hands were grabbing her breast while she was breastfeeding her baby.
Mad smile while she was squeezing that tit and observing the baby with eyes full of fire. She permitted her mother to hurt her, to squeeze her tit with those hot hands.

She let her.

Pretending that she does not notice

Until the baby started to throw up. The baby was puking. She was crying.
Her mother was shouting: Stop being so sensitive! I am trying to help you! Grow up for once! It is all you! You lost the plot! Stop blaming everybody and everything else! Grow up, what do you want from us old people?)
She woke up and said to her husband,

We won't be having any more children

He said, OK

After that the photo album is full of photos from their travels. Back then, everybody could travel without visas.
On every photo she is wearing big, black sunglasses, black dresses, standing next to different objects and different landmarks of different cities: Paris, Rome, Istanbul, Venice, Budapest...

*

Last time you wrote from the hospital
I could have imagined you lying on the bed. Your face pressed to the damp green wall, mumbling behind the closed blinds in between two dreams—

"I still dream about all that. I still dream about you
I see us running away from the police

The main street is a pile of mud

I am meeting you in front of a drugstore, we are talking about the places where palm trees grow
I remember a fairytale about 12 princesses that snuck out during the night to dance with twelve underworld princes

We danced

But those were not princes, there was nothing noble about it

I still do dream of the train, Trans-Sibirsk; we never managed to save enough money. I still do dream of an overdose. I imagine a death like that would feel like a sentence

Any sentence

Maybe even this one:
I still do dream of cheetahs running fast next to my bed. I can see them through a crack in the frame
You know, I do see it all now. How I managed to sabotage myself
But that numbness was all we knew and we wrap our lives around it
Like Christmas decorations around a dead pine tree:
Everybody knows it's dead

But it is nice to believe in it

The belief brings so much more than the disbelief. It brings us all together, like that mountain lamb roast, from which we will all get our share

Dead and uncommunicative

A piece of meat in our tight throats
Sorry I didn't mention that right away. I got used to blur.
To strategize. To dodge. To lie. To manipulate

Just in case

But that wasn't even a real death. It was a not so funny clown. It was losing all perspective

It was waste of time
A total waste of time

I remember:
You and then everything else

Edges, corners and faces
Ideas about such connections
Stretch as far back as
That day when the tooth was broken
By a bullet in the piece
Of this wild meat

That would be the essence of the cosmos, I thought

Chewing that hard, metal ball
With that hollow tooth
Strangely wrapped geometries unknown to my feet
Always
Led beyond the immediately obvious (what?)

Maximum number of edges
You have to traverse in order

To become a man
To become the man
To become a woman
To become the woman

And back again
And all over again
Again and again

All over covered in licks:
Warm sticky spring days are for wide open windows
All of them
Open them wide
Like you would spread your arms for a hug you haven't felt for
a long time

(I can't say I am missing you. It is good you left. You are a part
of me. That is. Your absence is in foundations of my being-
I created myself communicating with that absence)

The space is made of holes
For the breeze
For the flies
For atoms of grass
Broken eggshells
Fresh piss in the back corners
All up to your nostrils

Warm spring days are for staying in
Naked
Fucked
And nourished
In turns
But all I could think of was a writing on a piece of toilet paper
a toothless person handed to me, which I accepted with slight
nausea
While putting 10p in his empty paper cup:
"We are unlikely to have unlimited freedom of movement.
The holes are a luxurious ornament rather than exit.
The fruit importer might have a 1,000-dimensional problem
to deal with. If you have one or two, too hard to solve directly
just enter the casino of chance.

But if you want to win, it is always good to know a good bench,
a sofa, or a church to sleep in"

And that is the essence of happiness
Those warm moments
Of soft sadness and gentle repulsion
Those moments when you understand

I am in the state of happiness

At the end

Yes

*

You also said that you remember long walks with your mother
and men that were holding her hand and that weren't your
father

The neighbours were evil, such as any forced closeness
They were talking behind her back, spreading gossip, that
she was with all those men, just because they were buying her
drinks

Her husband and her mother stopped giving her money to
stop her drinking

You told me that you remember you were visiting her often in
hospitals

His father was picking her up often from police stations
She was aggressive when drunk

She was hiding her spirits everywhere behind, inside, above or
under just anything you could imagine—in perfume

bottles, Nutella jars, flowerpots, even in her beloved collection of lacrimariums

They would often find her, he said, in the snow in front of the building, all bloody and without consciousness

It is slippery around here these days, it can easily happen to just anybody to lose the ground under their feet and... and you roll down that hill, your father was saying to the neighbours

He made a handrail all by himself, next to the path leading to the building, just to make the point

You told me that your mother was entering the flat like she was running through a gunfire of shouting and accusations.

Her husband, her mother, the neighbours, the police the world—all of them against her.

She would dive in in her bed, with her clothes on but barefooted
Her feet green from sweating in cheap green shoes

You remembered those green feet

Green feet

Hanging from the bed

Sometimes she would throw up in her sleep

You told me that you still keep fruit in the same cracked crystal bowl. It cracked when she threw it at your father.
She missed him, the bowl fell onto the floor and cracked—
Fuck you and your wars, your revolutions, politics, parties, nostalgies, states, ideologies, fuck your everything!
If you were the winners, would you be the same, would you

think the same?
I hope so! I believe in that! her mother replied

She loved her father, my grandfather, you said; she would stroke his hand while he was just staring in the awe of non-recognition and shouting: THE MAGICAL JEWEL

You remembered how once as a 5-year-old boy you stayed alone with her in the flat
The flat was full of shadows and golden dusty fingers of light were caressing your mother's silky hair
She was lying still on top of the bed lighten and eternal
Unnatural
Like an exhibit in a cabinet of curiosities—The most beautiful sight you had ever seen
(She was dreaming a dream. It was winter. Big snow was snowing.
Soldiers were digging trenches through the streets.
Now in the dream she is she and she lies on her snow sledges in the garden, the snow is falling on top of her.
She imagines that she is a wounded partisan, in love with the supreme commander, the future dictator. Snow is dancing in front of her eyes, blossoming, plaiting into her eyelashes. Everything is peaceful. Finally.
Like the mouth of the world is smothered with a soft cotton cloth.
Peace.
Now in the dream, she is she but she is her mother as well (finally united) that watches her from her window. She sees her little girl, her minute body in red puffer jacket. She is lying on top of her sledges. The snow had already covered her)

You, the little boy, were pulling your mother's hand and crying,
Mummy, Mummy wake up!
Mummy wake up, please!
The little boy and his mother

His beautiful mother
While you were talking, I could imagine her, sitting on the toilet smoking, flicking her cigarettes into the ashtray that had been installed, on her demand, right next to the toilet paper holder

He told her that he saw her the last time when he was 17. They were arguing. They were arguing constantly. The neighbours were complaining constantly
They were arguing and he kicked her
He kicked her out of the flat
The next day she killed herself
Communists do not care about heaven and hell
That was her 7th attempt. It is not easy to kill yourself. But at the end you succeed, if you really want something and work on it.
She was cremated.
You were convinced that you saw one crow segregated from her flock, circling around the graveyard and over your head—her way to say, It is OK, don't worry!

They put her ashes on the brown shelf next to the big fat books by Marx, Engels, Hegel, next to her bronze bust.

You finished your story by saying that you remembered clearly that she loved to leave green lettuce in vinegar until it became all soft and soggy and only then she would eat it

*

The birds scattered across the metal furniture
The hospital corridors, beds
Flew all over the walls
And silenced at the spot
Where you have disappeared

*

It is silent

*

This silence is how this bird sings

*

Every time I wake up from my shallow dreams—
Like getting out from a warm, swampy river
You are there—perching elegantly on the frame of my bed
Your face in my palm, becomes real—
Warm pulsating handful of feathers
Dripping with gentle light.
The border is open every time you destroy those walls

The border is open now
So cross it—

The bird sings

Border is the skin, the place where you touch each other
Actually, it is that subatomic space
Between two bodies
Preventing them from the real touch.
The no man's land is real; it is the law of physics
And that is where I live
The border is longing for the other.
I long for you. How are you?
The bird sings
Where you disappeared there is a rupture
And in that rupture
The bird sings

Hide and Seek

The night was a free playground
The free territory
Proclaimed all over again with every sunset
They were waiting to fall
The Sun
The real
The visible
They were waiting for the logic to abdicate

And in the night you flow, all of stars and dreams

Under the soft neon
At the entrance into the concrete castle—its days numbered
Next to the billboard with plans for improvement, borders and futures

Through hard curtain of doll's bodies dressed up in loud textiles
Through dense formations of students in spasm of defending a drunken philosophical thesis (They grow their beard and shout, Change!)

Through monumental walls, immovable, smugglers—dragging their big bags with small wheels and through waves of strong smells of cooked food, she
Cuts
She cuts in the middle of a step
Have you seen him?

In the middle of a sentence
Have you seen him?
She interrupts hugs
Fights
She cuts the night, going from one person to another and
showing a photo of her son—
Have you seen him?
Her bad teeth and
Her facial features struggling to stay connected, to stay
wholesome. She is dividing herself into a multitude of
characters and she is coming back to herself again through the
Cracks in her dried face foundation
I bought him a silky Versace jumpsuit
It's all silk and
It's all purple and green
It's all gold
Have you seen him?
People like people in shoes like that
People like people in clothes like that
He just shimmers in smooth twists like a
King snake
Have you seen him?
Sssssssnake
King
Sssssswaying
Down the street
My king is missing for two weeks
I am looking for him
Have you seen him?
He is your age
He is 14
Her hand is losing the grip
She is constantly dropping the photo and picking it up from
the pavement—dirty fingernails
He is hiding
Have you seen him?
They have never seen him before

The two of them didn't know him
They were glad they were not him
Have you seen him?
Have you seen him?
Have you seen him?
Have you seen him?—It was echoing quieter and and farther and then merged with the city background noise

On the street, a commotion started—loud shouting and running
In front of them a man jumped out
The same guy who got them beer the other night
He was evaporating in anger
He pulled out a gun and he was
Flailing
Waving
Breathing like a bull
A marionette whose strings were pulled by the moon above his head
An aggressive object
A tool

He was throwing invisible confetti in sharp swings all around him
His head turning left and right
And then he saw them sitting on the stairs
Two white chubby faces, four big, dark eyes
Hey kids, long time no see... how's going? I salute you... Oh, you are scared of this?
He was turning his gun left and right in front of their noses.
Well that's a retard repeller, and you know what? It is empty!
Plus it's plastic, ok, maybe it is not plastic
Who cares!
Here, I will put it back!
He put the gun in his trousers and sat next to them
Do you have a cigarette?
She gave him a cigarette

I am nervous today—I was dreaming some crazy dreams—like
I am having a bath and my father enters the bathroom and I
give him a blowjob—He laughed hysterically
Can you imagine! What a dream!
Don't tell anyone!—he wasn't stopping with the laughter

Then he jumped on his feet and clapped his hands:
Right, where are we going?
You don't have a clue! Do you? You don't have a clue about
anything!
Let's go to a party!
I will look after you! You don't have to worry, he said, laughing
They allowed him to lead them
They followed him in complete silence
Solemnly
Like war prisoners that are walking their last 200 meters to the
wall where they will be executed

The fist in the air—
Freedom to the people!

And then they will fall down on their knees hit by bullets
You are just floating taken over by the stream that overwhelmed you
Your legs, your arms are not yours anymore
Your time is not your time
But you don't belong
And you will never

You are a tiny grain of freedom
And that might not be important at all, but who knows, it
might dissolve a knot in a final cosmic algorithm
In the car they were silent as well

She felt like all the future bad endings were being industrially manufactured right there at that very moment

His eyes were more on her than on the road. He was telling them about the party. It was in a house where some prostitutes from ex Eastern Bloc lived

It's cool, they are good girls, we all need money

Don't judge—just don't fall in love with one of them
Pussy has been devalued along with our national currency

We are all millionaires now
You can always find better

(THEY HAD HER UNDER THE THUMB
"Her value was decreasing with every new customer with every new owner. She was resold several times, amongst others, at war zones"

DOZENS INFECTED
"She was very young and pretty and it is right to presume that she was being mercilessly exploited in this dark business. It is known that her clients were businessmen, politicians, policemen...."

THE REGION IN PANIC
"She looked like an old woman. I had an impression that she doesn't weigh more than 50 grams. Terrifying image that will stay with me forever! Her life was put out by powerful and rich people that were turning their subjects into slaves. She was one of many. And she was only 21."

She was remembering the newspaper titles that were circulating those days: about a young prostitute that was thrown by her pimp, from a car in front of a hospital, in which she later died, in critical condition)

He wouldn't stop talking—We are all whores in this whorehouse
He was singing—We are all roses in this rosary
She was digging her nails into her palms: just please let nothing happens tonight
Just please, please let morning come quickly
Just please save us, Sun
She calmed down when she realised that he did take them to a party
And the party was good
Big flat, lots of people, and the music was fine
They separated from him right away and merged with the crowd
Happy they survived, and surviving
The disco ball was throwing little marbles of light rolling all through the space
Goldfish floating through the air
Two of them dancing, two bodies among other dancing bodies
She hangs around her neck
Slow advancing through the swamp
Heavy feet
Hank of dancers, knotted hands
The warmth in hips. It is good you are here
Everything makes sense when you are here
We are the stars in this film. We will win at the end. We will ride in the sunset that celebrates our victory. "The end" will glitter on the screen, over the fire of the dying day. We will be happy forever

The man approached her from behind and grabbed her by her shoulders then pressed his fingers into her muscles, and dragged them all the way to her hips

The hands stayed there prickling

Now, three of them were dancing squeezing her in the middle

He pulled her off the dance floor
Her friend was still dancing, disappearing among people and appearing again

She doesn't see, she doesn't stop, she is not giving up,
she dances
He turned her towards him
She didn't move
She didn't do anything
His wet face was changing colours in the rhythm of the music:
Green
Red
Gold
And his features melting and changing like he was all the faces at the same time
All faces that she knew, saw, alive and no longer existing, faces glowing in dreams, winking from the books, waving from the films. All people, the whole world at that moment crystalised in this not-that-funny clown, in this pathetic micro centre of power of this microcosmos

His tongue on her neck
The roughness of a man's face
He pinched the fat around her waist and start laughing:
I thought you were skinnier, but never mind, you know what we say: faces are selling pussies
(The same sentence her father told her once when he saw her in a mini skirt)

Come over here. He pushed her out of the flat, into
the elevator
They got out of the building
There was nothing out there
Just flat fields, and a highway and a moon softly rounded like a golden apple in the king's garden—a fairy tale she loved as a child

He pushed her on the ground—the partially burned cornfield
Sharp stabs cutting her back

("Girls like you are the worst once
they discover a dick"—she remembered a local junkie and how
he was shouting his wisdom every day to the girls coming out
from her school)

The moon was a golden scarab
Shiny vibrating wings
His hands on her belly
Hands on her buttocks
On her thighs
In her pants
Hands everywhere
He was soft, he was doing cocaine all night
Do something! I can't do all the work!
Move a bit!

Unsatisfied he was wanking himself violently
When he was ready he pulled down her jeans and he
entered her
All she could see was the moon, and a family story she once
heard or invented was unrevealing on the dark night sky above
her:

Just a week ago the roof was crunching under the weight of
snow
And never-ending
Lonely nights
Were filling her head with many unnecessary questions
Warmth of the house was silently facing the fact that behind
these walls
There was nothing
Just cold wilderness
And wilderness is something that does not belong to people
Snow glittered in the moonlight

Hills blinking with silver shine
Like all men did, her husband went to a town to work
Women were waiting and looking after children

Once, just before the dawn
Her child, that was sleeping next to her
Woke her up and whispered,
Mummy, look!
In the corner of the room, under the beam of the moonlight, two mice were dancing
Holding each other by the paws
Making small steps
To the left
And to the right
One step ahead
One step behind
And then round and round:
Movements of shadows multiplied by the misleading and convincing force of the Moon
A curious happening that they were involved with by coincidence and insomnia
She shuddered, thinking about events uncaused by a decision or even a mistake, Situations bigger than people and their desires
Self-happening of the world—

All those things that are going on without us, and more and more without us
As we are getting old
She looked through the window
It was still snowing
Quick and thick snow
The next day through the heavy wooden door and from the snow curtain
Emerged a face of a man
The child asked hidden behind her skirt,
Who is this man, mummy?

It is your father
Now he was gone again, but the spring was making things easier
Everything is always easier in the sun
She enjoys gardening in the warmth, she knows well each plant
This day was going to be long
She felt that from the dawn
And decided to visit her parents on the other side of the mountain
The path was passing through a forest
That most of the local people were trying to avoid
The young do not care for old women's bloodcurdling stories
About forest demons
Creatures of dark needs
Lurking in the shadows
Talking animals
And enchanted humans who there
Lost their sanity and soul
One of the most known stories was that one about an old man and a goat kid:

Once upon a time an old man bought a goat kid. He spent all day at the market and he was tired, so he decided he would go home via a shortcut that led through the forest. As he was stepping deeper into the forest, he didn't want to admit that by each step he was regretting more he chose that way. He was cooing to the kid, trying to encourage himself:

Don't you worry, grandad's little kid… don't you worry, grandad's kid!
All of the sudden, the goat stopped, looked at the old man with its red blood eyes and started to bleating in A horrifying voice, Bleee, bleee, graaaandaaaad's liiitleeee kiiiiid, Bleee, bleee, graaaandaaaad's liiitleeee kiiiiid

The old man started to run, and he was running and running until he fell completely exhausted near his house. From then on, he was irreversibly connected to the forest's dark forces, and he saw things in his head no man should see, and he knew things no man should know

At a moment when the dark need overwhelmed him, and he started to kill animals with great pleasure and to suck their blood, yearning more every day warm human blood, he decided to leave his village and to take his own life in the forest that disturbed his mind. He went to the forest, and nobody saw him ever again. That is, even if somebody did see him, they didn't live to tell.

She was young and strong
So she went
Went through the new grass
Holding her child

(Hills under the snow and dark trees. He didn't shave his beard nor cut his hair for forty days*)

The sky was so blue
Big
So close and full of insects and birds

(We think that he killed the cat. He said that she was ominous; he said that she became greedy and left, because she thought she could find something better. But she was wrong, he said, look around us!

There is nothing. Nobody. No men, no demons. No bush whisperers
He talks about that constantly. He knows he is annoying. He knows that we are afraid. He is waiting for the pretext. We are silent, looking forward for him to go outside)

Slowly, the light sprout bushes
Started to be replaced with old corpulent trees

Tufts of fog winding among the trees
Drops
Of moisture caught in spider webs: diamond jewels thrown all across the wood

(He is outside shouting at the goats and throwing snow at the hens. He is old and slow. Something is dripping on my hair: pieces of meat are drying on hooks, and the grease is dripping on the floor.
We hate him.)

It was much darker now
Half-opened mushrooms were whitening on the ground
There were no insects

Animals were announcing their presence shrieking in half-human voices

The river was louder as she was approaching it
In spite all the scary stories she felt close to this river

Every time she passed through
She would throw one
Pebble
Over her head into the water for every wish she had

(Then we would go out for a walk and sunbathe on a rock uncovered by snow.
And then, in the warmth of the sun, we would feel sorry for him.
My mother would say, On one hand, I do understand him, since she is gone, there is nobody to serve
him in his kingdom of one servant.
And what is a king without his subjects?)

She closed her eyes, made a wish, and threw a pebble into the water

She opened her eyes
And at that moment she thought she saw somebody
It can't be!
She closed
And
Opened
Her eyes again
And changed the wish holding tightly onto her child
Yes, definitely! Somebody is hiding behind that tree
The only visitors around here were slightly lost peasants or hunters
But they would just say hello and keep on with their business
A man in a suit in this wilderness was scarier than all the stories she had ever heard

The border was close
The new war was close
The old war was close
Aggression culminating in the air
Dripping

Insects getting crazier before the rain
She knew well the pattern of all horrific stories:
When somebody deserts the usual path
Or
Is persistent to expose something that is hidden
Forbidden
That person is being pushed directly
Onto the front line where the forces which are forming our universe
Are weighing up their strength
It is discouraging that belief that anyone who breaks a rule, that person will be punished
And on the other hand, it is a bit true that life can really become a horrific scenario if one insists
On unnecessary information
She would pretend she didn't see him

Don't worry, he wouldn't harm us
She was whispering to the child as they were getting closer
The forest path was leading to the tree
If she left the path
He would knew that she saw him
The stranger in the hat was moving slowly around the tree as she was approaching
One her step ahead
One his step behind
He knew that he was seen
And she knew that he knew
They were just following the rules of this weird game:
I am like hidden, you are like not seeing me
I will not hurt you as long as you show clearly that you are not interested in what am I doing here
The time has stopped
They entered eternity
Yellow changed sky
Without birds
Slopes under the musky smelling moss
The steady sound of the river
She could see clearly turquoise lichen on the rocks
Tiny fractures
In the tree barks
And
Fast ants going up and down
The rustling of the dry leaves was unpleasantly loud
I am like not seeing you. You are like hidden
I am like hidden. You are like not seeing me
Don't worry we are almost out of here, she said, kissing the child
Drops
Of
Moisture
Were
Unhurriedly
Sliding

Down
The
Plants
And
Drops
Of
Her
Sweat
Down
Her
Naked
Neck
The child was asleep in her arms

(Maybe he didn't kill the cat, after all. Look there in that snow: those are cat footprints!)

When he was finished, he rolled on his back, placing her face on his chest
She could hear his heartbeat
The corn stalks were still stabbing her back
He checked his hands, they were covered with blood
He started to laugh: Surprise, surprise...
First time

There, he stroked her hair—
You are dirty now just like I am

Just like everybody else is
Now you are one of us
She got up. Tried to make her clothes clean again
He zipped up his trousers, lit a cigarette and went back to the party, giving a sign with his fingers that he would call her, and sending her a kiss, pouting his mouth

(You will die from lung cancer; your system will sabotage itself—mutation of cells

I am a mutated cell of society
A grain of freedom)

She is coming back home. Always does. Always home. And tall trees and mad early birds like illogical conclusions are starting to shout

Before she understands the wholesome meaning (I am dragging myself around), there must be a process (jugglers are playing with small fires, bouncing on smooth, stone streets) of creating of that meaning
The most important thing now, is that you can leave,
She thought
(That I can leave, that everybody can leave)
She was waiting for the first bus and for the dark to glue off from the burnt fields. She was waiting for everything to end and for everything to start from the beginning

But it started when it started

Birds' shrieks ringing in the loneliest place: the-just-before-dawn
Everything is better without the sound. Turn it off!
People started to gather in front of shops waiting for milk, to gather in front of embassies, to put their old coats smelling of lavender and sour cabbage on the cardboard boxes

Something might be sold today
The misted bus windows, the finger drawn smeared heart.
Crossing the bridge—she observes couples, eyes open wide as a child's: neon white tights leaking through his fingers

She observes people
People live under the bridges. People live on boats, in houses,

and on mountains and next to the sea. People live in wars, in
armistices, on margins, on streets. People live everywhere

Anyway, anyhow
People live

Back home, she brushed her teeth and had a bath
She couldn't fall asleep
She was covered in cuts and bruises
She liked that
The cut is only something you get when you play rough—
with yourself
When you fall hard
Because the floors are slippery, it is hard to find balance
Now, the pain is the purest feeling. All the rest is mixed with
repulsion
Now when she knows things no person should know.
But then again, everything is there to be known
There are no free playgrounds
And her desires will always stink of cigarettes and alcohol, her
desires will always be murky, of the night, her desires won't be
reading books or writing poetry, her desires will be two-sided,
entangled and explosive, drowning in far-away seas, hunting
intensity in the vacuum after a gunshot

Her desires will always scratch the skin to the dark, to the raw,
to the things that hurt

"Now you are one of us"
Her fingers smelling of bubble bath and bleach
Her fingers
Touching
A touch wants another touch, that leads somewhere: I am going
I am going towards me
And this body is a crystal
A diamond
The pleasure of shining

And this pleasure of shining is mine
This pleasure of shining—that is me
She fell asleep finally with her hand still in her pajamas, she slept sound and long
Her mother, woke up early as always, came to her bedroom to check if she came back home
She put another blanket over her, the days began to get cold
For few moments she was observing her daughter sleeping—
Asleep like this.
All soft.
All feathery and new.
When she sleeps like this, she still looks like a child -

Mummy's little girl

---

* It is customary not to cut the hair, nor to trim the beard, for 40 days when a family member dies.

Do Your Thing, Storm

The weather forecast was wrong again.
It should have been a nice day. And it was in the morning.
Now it is obvious that the sky above the park edge is deeply gray, and the grayness is growing
Approaching
A tiny drop of rain on her nose—she decided not to notice and another one and another

Maybe it is not rain, maybe some other water

Her jeans were unpleasantly cold, soaked with sticky lemonade.

One of the children spilled their bottle all over her

Each year children's birthdays were becoming more and more a Beyond-control chaotic happening. A fight club, survival camp. Exercise of nerves, patience, reflexes and logistics

Now she, the captain of this ship, saw the storm on the horizon.

What shall she do with the sailors?

With wild sailors that love open sea and get crazy in closed spaces.
Where is the closest (covered) harbour?

(There are spans of calmness, of vast flat seas
The whole day before she had her first child was like that:
Her enormous belly
Her inflated body
Enjoyably inert
Suspended on a chair
In their new, cleaned kitchen, watching the night through the terrace doors
Warm wind slowly moving the curtains
The washing machine is on
Its rhythm mesmerizing, in warm sync with the house breathing
Grinding the time into a vision of the future
Future
So soft
Then the pain arrived
The unstoppable merciless mechanism
Give me some pills!
I believe in science!
The next thing she remembers is her waking up in a hospital bed
She never accepted that
She never accepted what they told her she became that day
A mother!
The moment you had your child the hospital staff would just call you: MOTHER
You lose your name you became—Mother
New woman, old name
Hey, mother, time to wake up!
All of the sudden, she wasn't she anymore but a mother!
It felt like that day she reached perfection, and all of the sudden somebody put on her a cursed costume of that mythological creature called MOTHER

That creature grinning from big books dedicated to psycho-analytic theories.
Problematic creature, the creature of the problem-

tamers unable to tame their own creation
The costume that would grow into her skin, into her bones,
squeezing her intestines

To get rid of it one must not feel pain or shame
To take it off you have to peel off parts of your skin, of your
bones, to rip yourself inside

And emerge disfigured, reshaped into something else, but just
yours, newly self-built

Stained pajamas, cockroaches running towards dark corners
like broken pieces of her personality running away from this
motherly light, babies crying

She was in and out of dreams
Each time more aware of that storm, of that mother that was
growing inside of her
Mother growing. Growing. Mother.
We will have a ball, you and me—MOTHER

She thought when she first saw the face of her baby)

A mother of one of the children standing next to her for more
than an hour, and talking about something that kept getting
lost in the thunder of the children's voices

The only thing that she was able to notice was the red lipstick on
her teeth. And the smell of eucalyptus, floating about her lips.
Her jeans
Wet
Sticky
The person, she is there, she is not going away
She is talking, she is not stopping
Children—noise making
The grayness is approaching

The drops of rain, more frequent
Wind
Focus!
Think!
She bites her nails, decides to move the birthday party inside the nearest cafe

She is calling the children
Taking them by their sticky little hands
Sailors, let's go!
The smell of upcoming storm excites
Promising something new
A child of the mother next to her was teasing her about her accent: And in which language are you talking? Martian?

She replied with the most serious smile: Listen, my child, when you learn to speak my language as good as I am speaking yours,
I will buy you a beer, OK?

The child's mother was feeling uncomfortable
She was giving a prolonged smile to the confused girl
She doesn't like that child
In a Hollywood film they would love each other by the end of it, after the initial disagreements, through the conflict they would learn about the other and about themselves
The meeting would transform them

But in this case that would not happen

She had enough of transformations

She doesn't like that child, and she doesn't like her mother, she decided like that, she doesn't have patience anymore, she cannot forgive any more

Especially at the end of the day
At the end of the day, she doesn't like people in general
She just wants to take her child and be alone with him
But her child wants to be with other children
Let the children go with children

Let them go

(Very often she listens to recordings of snowstorms
Hours and hours of snowstorms
She fantasies about desolate wastelands
About snow
About places where, there is nobody.
She listens to the storms that have female names, she likes that:

Eleanor is causing traffic chaos
Eleanor is disturbing trains and airplanes
Eleanor is throwing debris from beaches to the roads and coastal properties
Eleanor is a consequence of human greed and arrogance
For some Eleanor means revenge
Eleanor breaks
Legs
Heads
Fences
Walls
Branches
For some Eleanor is just a hubris of destiny, some instant karma
Eleanor threatens capital investments
For some Eleanor is awakening of global consciousness, but still
Eleanor won't convince everybody in global warming
Eleanor is then a conspiracy theory
Eleanor
Eleanor blows, twists, she loses control
Eleanor is uprooting trees and electric cables, deconstructs the communication systems.
For some, Eleanor is a pure coincidence and proof of an

impersonal Universe without emotions, but
Eleanor is angry and there is a high possibility (80%) she will become angrier

Eleanor is dying above the Baltic
To disappear like that, after all, in thin air above a faraway sea)

In the park, there was an art installation celebrating peace in the world: a big, all-white chessboard
The rain started to fall heavily

Almost all of the kids were inside the park cafe
Two children, her own and those of the mother that would not stop talking, were arguing at the middle of the chess board

They were battling over one white pawn, even though there were 16 white pawns

They were pushing each other, crying
Everybody wanted exactly that white pawn on exactly that white field

It is mine! No, it is not! It is mine!

Move away! You move away!
That is mine! I came first! No, I came first!

It seems that war is in human blood, isn't it? She turned to the child's mother; she was nodding her head, laughing
They managed to calm down their children and to take them to the cafe
In one moment, you just let the chaos grow, let them do whatever they want

(There are spans of calmness, of vast flat seas
Like when she observes her child while eating:
His soft cheeks, big silky curls

He is telling her with all seriousness that they are having
yogurt on Wednesdays at school
And she is watching him, and she sees the small new world that
is growing and in which
Yoghurt is eaten on Wednesdays
Probably fruit yoghurt, and all smells of strawberries
Miniature galaxies that float under his skin
And he sparkles
Glows like one magnificent day of tomorrow
She watches him and sees that independent future world with
its own rules
Shaping right now in front of her
She kisses his hair
And that is love)

They connected over the war at the chessboard that symbolises
Peace—that was a too good opportunity not to abandon her
decision about disliking, and she ordered a round of drinks

And now she saw her for the first time—her tense face and
painted on eyebrows—she did that well.
Unlike her daughter she had strong foreign accent

I came from the war, she said

She liked how, in this city, there were so many stories, not just
one, not just yours, you are not stuck with just your same old
broken story

In this city, you get dissolved, you stop, you get away, finally
They were talking, drinking, exchanging traumas and
symptoms

Laughing—the foamy avalanche when you open a bottle of
champagne

The pressure becomes sparkling

My war is better than yours!

Yes, your war is better than mine!

My is some old, obsolete, crappy little war nobody cares about anymore except the ones that lost everything, except the ones that lost themselves

Slimy war without heroes, without big ideas, if there is any other kind war ever!

Yours is better: More people. More bombs. New technologies. Robots. Drones. More deaths. More refugees. More everything

Your war is the new black

The brand-new story in the town
And then another war will come
And then another one
There is always the next war
The storm was beating against the windows of the cafe
The children were putting ketchup, mustard, salt in their soft drinks

The food was falling on the floor, sliding from the chins
They will soon take them home
They will see each other again—I am glad I have found you

(Many years later, she will roam around streets bursting with colour and plentitude)
In a faraway country
She will not be able to understand the objects
Remembering those visions
Of street boys leaning on hot walls in vivid colours, somewhere far away (not existing faraway) where palm trees are growing

And big salty waves are washing the avenues of freedom

Those boys those girls are actually overworked
Factory employees
The heat
The mosquitoes
The buzzing of the machines

Cheap production for cheap consumption

The poor for the poor

Our poverties are working against us
My poverty against your poverty

That is how they keep us in this rink:
"Happiness is small things."

And then you can't refuse because happiness is this cheap shirt
Happiness is those broken plastic parts
Happiness must be new
Happiness does not last long
Happiness falls apart after two days of loving
Happiness is being proud for being randomly born in some random part of the world
After all happiness is when you eat and drink and fuck
But admit deep down
You want it
I want it
Deep down you don't want to refuse
To deny yourself that slight possibility of wealth
Refusing is cutting yourself off from the way to the stars

Like no dream is possible without hierarchy

No hierarchy, no dream

Happiness is not small things. Happiness are the biggest things

(But they don't have anything to do with all of this)

Small things are just a token
A promise of a happy end

A promise that you will, someday, somehow, rule this world

And she will have a strong panic attack in front of a furniture shop because of the furniture
Endless combinations for endless scenarios
When in fact there is just one
Because of her reflection in the glass window
Because of
"What is wrong with you?" is now an ontological question
Incurable disease
"Since when do you feel like this?"
Since before I was born
Dysfunctional unit of society—the subversive unit of the system
And that is where I am winning
In this ubiquitous omnipresence

Being subversive now hides in small crevices in reality—
Persistent headache of a dishwasher that intensifies

Hair-thin rupture in a family porcelain cup that branches
Error in the stitch
Error in steps
Just an error
I am an error
The disorder is multiplying. The disorder inside of me.
There is a storm, the storm is growing inside of me

Do your thing, storm

All that is raw
Now is covered with petals

Do your thing storm

Disenchant us
Make us flow through the ruptures, through the bars
Let us shine from joyfulness
Raw and fragile, let us flourish in gentleness
In softness
Make us want
Make us love
Make me love

(Myself the way I wanted to be loved by others)

Do your thing, storm
Make me love
More
Always more, and forever)

The storm was getting wild outside, the children were getting wild inside

The woman finished her story: And where are you from?
I don't remember you mentioned it, exactly.

(Who is the lovely mother of my little soldier?
The most magnificent woman I have ever seen?
The producer of powerful magic?
The talented thinker with whom you were able to brush through (like through a mare's silky hair) the world of literature, over a civilised dinner, like you never did with anyone before?
A seductive cook and a housewife?
Warm and patient she does not play—
She is too mature for games

The talented storyteller, with her mesmerising voice she puts eagles to sleep
She is natural
Is that me?
Am I still me? Now I have the wondrous talent of this creature that squeezes her juices to oil with gentleness hard gears that are breaking spines and balls?

Is this my the most perfect manifestation and the name of that manifestation is mother?

One might say that a language we understand is the language we love and while threading on this slippery texture rushing like a bull on ice towards the warm and wet reward of understanding
So desperately in need for understanding
But I don't understand, I don't hear, because through that word MOTHER, thunders some other language that I am fluent in

The dark chatter of that Other
Under pressure. Insane. Unknown. That was growing inside of itself, through hard concrete creating its own deep continent

In my language we don't have a word for Motherland, just Fatherland
But even if there was a word, Motherland is always something different
The only word that means a place connected to a mother is a swear word: Materina
You use it when you want to say somebody to fuck off: Go back to your mother's (cunt)
Also means a faraway shit place nobody wants to go to
But upside down Fatherland is Materina, waiting on the other side of the mirror
Materina, that favourite swear word

Let's just all fuck off into freedom! Materina, the free territory!

After all, we are all from that place

At the end of the day, all of us earn the utmost we can carry, and I knew I could carry the body of this woman, and that woman was me, her square geometrical body, her sticky syntax made of full fat calories, underarms unwanted and wobbly, her hot, pulsating vowels, her spiky consonants, her linguistics dripping with miniature explosions blowing away hardened ways

I knew I could carry her through the pores
To undress her from the needs of others, to just hers, naked perfect skin, to pull her from under the carpet right to the end of the old world, right to the demolition of every decency.

Decent for whom?

At that moment I knew. I could carry her. I was ready to face the earnings... (if only)

She finished her drink in a professional elegant sway and said, I am from Materina

ACKNOWLEDGEMENTS

Thank you my Martin, thank you Cousin and Lady, thank you Little Friend.

Thank you Sophie.

Thank you Robert Lundquist and Rushika Wick for reading, editing and believing in this book even when I didn't.

Thank you Tamara Suskic and Tatjana Suskic for the cover photo and for being my permanent inspiration.

Thank you Sanja Maricic and my mother and my father without whom nothing would happen in the first place not even this book.

Thank you Nina Zivancevic for being my poetry guide and "shaman". Thank you Mihajlo Jovanović, Daisy Steele, Snezana Mocovic, Kirsty Allison, Heathcote Ruthven and Sam Hacking for making me feel me and that my poetry belongs somewhere.

Thank you Manja Ristic for "all that poetry/life jazz" we've been through together.

Thank you Milan Milosavljevic for all the support and the design for Materina T-shirts! Thank you Jovana Backovic for turning *Materina* into a music piece.

Thank you Dolla, Eloise, Amy, Joanna, Jess, Ben, Bean, Riley, Ali, Garry, Monty, Denise, Laura H., Sofie, Cindy, Rachel, Fariha, Dorothy, Asha, Sara, Rebecca, Sabina, Michelle, Yasmine, Bella, Steph, Sandra, Vanessa, Laura F., Paul, Martha, Ange, Fallon, Paolo, John.

ALSO AVAILABLE FROM VERVEPOETRYPRESS.COM

Eighty Four:
Poems on Male Suicide, Vulnerability, Grief and Hope

With an introduction from editor Helen Calcutt

Eighty Four was originally a new anthology of poetry on the subject of male suicide in aid of CALM. Poems were donated to the collection by Andrew McMillan, Salena Godden, Anthony Anaxogorou, Katrina Naomi, Ian Patterson, Caroline Smith, Carrie Etter, Peter Raynard, Joelle Taylor, while a submissions window yielded many excellent poems on the subject from hitherto unknown poets we are thrilled to have been made aware of.

We hope this book will shed light on an issue that is cast in shadow, and which is often shrouded in secrecy and denial. If we don't talk, we don't heal and we don't change. In Eighty Four we are all talking. Are you listening?

Available in paperback:
ISBN: 978 1 912565 13 9
188 pages • 216 x 138 • 56 poems
£11.99

And on eBook:
ISBN: 978 1 912565 79 5
£6.99

ALSO AVAILABLE FROM VERVEPOETRYPRESS.COM

Impure Thoughts
Golnoosh Nour

Impure Thoughts is a pamphlet of brand new work from twice Polaris Shortlisted author, Golnoosh Nour.

'Riotous and fizzing with language, the poetry of Golnoosh Nour boldly explores what it is to be utterly alive and ecstatically, yet complicatedly, in desire.' –Richard Scott

'Impure Thoughts is a dizzying dance through impurity's several selves. Half bal masqué, half Grand Guignol, Nour confronts the limits of desire with an almost uncanny intensity of focus. Even at their most tender and elegiac these poems tremble with the white-hot heat of libidinal energy and gleam with oracular fury.' –Fran Lock

Available in paperback:
ISBN: 978 1 913917 21 0
36 pages • 210 x 148 • 20 poems
£8.50

ABOUT VERVE POETRY PRESS

Verve Poetry Press is a quite new and already prize-winning press that focused initially on meeting a local need in Birmingham - a need for the vibrant poetry scene here in Brum to find a way to present itself to the poetry world via publication. Co-founded by Stuart Bartholomew and Amerah Saleh, it now publishes poets from all corners of the UK - poets that speak to our city's varied and energetic qualities and will contribute to its many poetic stories.

Added to this is a colourful pamphlet series, many featuring poets who have performed at our sister festival - and a poetry show series which captures the magic of longer poetry performance pieces by festival alumni such as Polarbear, Matt Abbott and Imogen Stirling.

The press has been voted Most Innovative Publisher at the Saboteur Awards, and has won the Publisher's Award for Poetry Pamphlets at the Michael Marks Awards.

Like the festival, we strive to think about poetry in inclusive ways and embrace the multiplicity of approaches towards this glorious art.

www.vervepoetrypress.com
@VervePoetryPres
mail@vervepoetrypress.com